Finding Mom:
A Daughter's Rite of Passage

By Nancy Hadley, Ed. D.

Garden Publishing Company, LLC

Finding Mom: A Daughter's Rite of Passage
ISBN: 978-0-9833377-5-1

Copyright © 2014 by Nancy Hadley
Interior design and formatting by Grant Hill
Cover art and design by Gail Kirkham

Published by Garden Publishing Company
10403 US Highway 87 North
Sterling City, Texas 76951

This book or parts of this book may not be reproduced in any form, stored in a retrieval system, or transmitted in any form by any means - mechanical, electronic, photocopying, recording, or otherwise - without prior written permission by the author, except as provided by the United States of America copyright law.

Printed in the United States of America.

Garden Publishing Company

Dedication and Thanks

This book is dedicated to my family and to the memory of my beloved mother, Mary Jane Willis Darby, November 12, 1922-May 5, 2010.

I want to thank my dear friend, Gail Kirkham, for editing this book and for allowing me to use one of her paintings for the cover art.

In addition, I want to thank Kevin McSpadden and Grant Hill for their invaluable contributions to this book in editing and formatting respectively. I am grateful for the time they invested, the encouragement they provided, and the detailed consideration they gave to this project.

Table of Contents

Introduction		7
Chapter 1	The Crisis	13
Chapter 2	Survival	21
Chapter 3	Adaptation	29
Chapter 4	Depression	35
Chapter 5	Custodial Care	43
Chapter 6	A New Home	55
Chapter 7	Acceptance	63
Chapter 8	Endurance	67
Chapter 9	Rite of Passage	71
Chapter 10	Suffering	75
Chapter 11	Inheritance	81
Epilogue		87

Introduction

It was late one night when I got the call from Mom. We talked every day to "touch base," so when she called again, I knew something was up. She had not been feeling well, spending more time resting on the couch than usual. She was very concerned about the way she was feeling. I asked her if we should go to the emergency room right then and she declined. However, she agreed to call the doctor in the morning. The next morning the doctor decided she should go to the emergency room. She insisted on driving herself, so my brother, Drew, and I met her there.

Mom was admitted to the hospital with a heart attack. After the tests were conducted, the doctors told us she had a 50-50 chance of having another massive, life-threatening heart attack within a week. In their estimation, it wasn't a matter of "if" but "when," and the "when" was soon. So after discussing her options, Mom consented to the quadruple by-pass surgery they recommended. Although she had suffered a stroke-like event resulting in an occluded carotid artery months before, the surgeons assured us they would take precautions to handle this complication to the surgery. She was petrified of having a debilitating stroke but could not live with the threat of an impending heart attack looming over her head. Mom's high blood pressure had kept her blood circulating despite the blocked carotid artery, but when they lowered her blood pressure to conduct the by-pass repair, she suffered her worst nightmare, a catastrophic stroke. Although her heart was repaired, at 81 she was left paralyzed on her right side and unable to speak.

Our family was used to tragedy, as Dad was abruptly taken in a plane crash at the age of 51. I was 22 at the time and Mom was 48. Mom battled back from this devastating blow. With only a high school education, she managed to turn the modest insurance money she received from Dad's death into a simple but comfortable life through educating herself about the stock market. Before the surgery Mom was astoundingly vibrant and independent, even though she had chronic high blood pressure, kidney problems, a bout with melanoma, a deep vein thrombosis, and partial colon removal. She was a beautiful, cheerful, and vibrant woman who had been a fiercely independent servant of her family and friends; the personification of motherhood; the epitome of selfless service. She was an amazing woman.

None of us were prepared for the ordeal we were to endure as a result of this tragic turn of events. We

Introduction

were faced with an extremely ominous situation. The stroke left Mom speechless and flaccid on her dominant side with questionable recognition. She became dependent instead of independent, a position she fought and openly disdained. It was abundantly clear to all of us how Mom felt about any type of helpless role, and a living will documented her wishes to forego any heroic efforts to preserve her life at all costs.

At first we were concerned with whether or not Mom would ever get out of the hospital. She finally awoke enough to squeeze our hands with recognition. It was a breakthrough to be able to converse with her as she gained the strength to nod her head "yes" or "no." I rejoiced the day I came in to find her sitting up.

Then there were what seemed to be endless hurdles, the first of which was swallowing. Would she have to endure a feeding tube or could she manage to pass the swallowing test? Fortunately, she passed that test. She got an infection in her leg incision that took months to heal with a wound V.A.C. machine that promoted healing through the negative pressure of a vacuum. At one point we thought we were going to have to amputate her dormant foot as it got infected. We dodged that bullet as well. After several stints in rehab facilities and a stretch in a nursing home, Mom finally landed in an assisted living facility with the compassionate help of a hired caregiver who became a dear friend to all of us.

Mom lived six years and three months after her surgery. I was fifty-five at the beginning of the ordeal, teaching at a university with a wonderful and supportive husband of twenty-one years, a daughter married just two years prior, and a son in his first year of college. It was the first year of my empty nest that my life was radically interrupted. I had driven hard through life myself, passing milestones such as a bachelor's degree, loss of father, marriage, first child, divorce, single motherhood, second marriage, second child, master's degree, doctorate, professional accomplishments, and marriage of first child. To be honest I was looking forward to coasting for a while, not strapping on another burden. Not only was I in a front row seat to witness Mom living out her worst nightmare in excruciating pain, but my life was irreparably altered. I found myself catapulted into a daily regimen of caring for my Mom, and I struggled to cope. I guess I had the best of situations because Mom lived in the same town, as did my only sibling, Drew, who shared the care-giving duties, took the financial load, and most importantly, cradled me during the endless job of deciding what to do next. Despite the enduring support of my husband, friends, and family, I felt the yoke a daughter feels when her Mom suddenly becomes helpless.

    I found solace in writing and reflecting through this trial. Writing about it somehow transferred part of the burden to the paper. Once on paper, I could try to make sense of it. I first entitled the journal, "Losing Mom", but later revised the title to "Finding Mom." But Mom wasn't the only person I found. I ended up finding myself as well. Through this experience I not only faced her dreadful experiences but uncovered some of my own skeletons.

It was a rite of passage for me, and through it I made my way out of the habitual responses that had become the norm in my rapport with my Mom. I had somehow missed a defining event in my mother-daughter relationship that would have made me feel like I was on equal footing with her as a woman. I knew my Mom loved and respected me, but we never talked about things like that, and I was trapped in still feeling like a child in my mother's presence despite my age and entry into motherhood myself. In other arenas I was fully vested in adulthood, but with Mom, I just never seemed to move out of my childhood, not only in how I felt when I was around her, but also in how I reacted to her comments about me. Through this tragic turn of events, we finally broke out of the mold which had been the region of captivity of our relationship. At 55 I gained equal footing not only for my sake but for hers as well. My rite of passage happened without words or a special event, but it was the perfect confirmation that had eluded me. The irony was that I sought Mom's verbal approval all of my life and finally received it when she was unable to speak.

Finding Mom chronicles my trek and the epiphanies along the way. It was written during the six plus years of Mom's illness and bears the marks of raw emotions beginning with the crisis and ending with completion. I wouldn't recommend the circumstances, but I would never trade the journey.

Chapter 1

The Crisis

The crisis stage was characterized by anxious waiting. The days morphed together, creating a blur of emotion. Tears ebbed and flowed in waves as we huddled together around Mom. It was amazing to me how exhausting sitting in a hospital room became. How could that be? Continuous emotional exhaustion was far more devastating than physical exhaustion. It was constant and unrelenting. Repeated restless or sleepless nights drained my reserves. Fresh air was at a premium during the staleness of confinement.

The routine pace of the hospital staff clashed with my inner state of emergency, yet I knew my panic would be replenished daily by another emergency, then another. I did so appreciate the gentle hugs from the trained professionals who specialize in not only healing but ministering as well. I knew they were fueled by the occasional miracle I hoped to see. I was blessed by several of those professionals who took the time to pause and connect with reassurance. The knowing eye contact, the surprising hug, the extra information, the corrected expectations, and the sounding board for doubts provided moments when some of my heartache was transferred and shared like a discharge of static electricity. Waiting and trusting were the most difficult hurdles to clear during this stage. Not knowing was the cross to bear.

Our normal routines stopped as we settled into the drill dictated by ICU, a foreign land to most but an unwitting home in crisis. ICU had zones, separated by locked doors. The ICU waiting area was where the families were held hostage. Visitors would come and go, but families stayed, awaiting any word from behind the doors. Entrance behind the doors was granted during visiting hours, but I noticed that once you were in, nobody ran you out. The trick was to make sure someone was "in" at all times so that the sporadic doctor appearances could be intercepted and the life-line of information secured, deciphered, then disseminated. Information became more vital than food or drink, and we scrambled for any morsel.

As the days droned on, it felt like we were drafted into a macabre play, in which we were dealt a role and required to perform. Mom assumed the unwelcomed, silent role in this play, and my brother, Drew, and I were unwillingly thrust into the lead roles. We felt like we were supposed to know what to do, yet we found no script. Drew and I reacted with spontaneous, impromptu responses. In reflecting on this drama, I find it interesting how important the supporting roles and cameo appearances from various people became an integral part of the plot determination for me. Each person I encountered shaped my reality, and I pondered their role in my drama.

Were you a volunteer in the ICU waiting room who organized the chaos and indoctrinated the newcomers with the routines? The veteran families knew the drill, but the newcomers were unsure and confused. Your reassuring voice calmed my nerves. I was grateful for your presence because your numbers were few, especially on the weekends. You crept behind the doors like a scout behind enemy lines and smuggled me in between visiting hours. I hoped you knew your service could not be measured.

Were you part of another extended family sitting in the ICU waiting room when I was behind the doors? You were the life-line to the friends who were anxious for some word about Mom. You and our loved ones exchanged vital updates that kept hope alive. If you answered the phone in the absence of an official, you became part of our family, part of our hope. We tried to reciprocate and become involved in your crisis as well. News was passed freely as we came to trust one another. We celebrated good news together and hugged on receipt of bad news. I felt a special bond with each of your families. Shared pain seemed easier to bear.

Were you the efficient nurse, the unbending rule keeper, the one who systematically cared for my Mom? Were you the technician who came in the room and raised your eyebrow because of illegal cell phone usage? Were you the aide who ignored my desperate plea to open the door early in the morning because of regulations? Or were you the nurse who kept me out, missing the doctor's visit, the efficient one, the one in control? If you were among these, you made my journey more difficult.

Were you one of the compassionate nurses? I am grateful that there were many. I looked forward to your shift. Your accessibility and abundant supply of information kept me going. You asked me how I was doing and assured me that my questions were welcomed. You graced me with lingering eye contact and a well-timed hug. You brought an unsolicited food tray for me to eat. I felt your compassion, and I knew this was your calling, not your job.

Were you one of several colleagues who took over and organized my work so that I could feel comfortable being away? You each played an immeasurable role in my crisis because you took the weight of my responsibilities and shouldered them for me. I worried about being away, and you allowed me to focus all of my energies on the crisis at hand. The camaraderie we shared was permanently enriched.

Were you the friend who had stood in my shoes or the prayer warrior who lifted me up? The tears in your eyes and your knowing hug momentarily dissipated my turmoil. You nurtured my spirit with unseen, yet very real strength. The meals you brought to my family fed our needs and nourished our spirits. I could not seem to eat the food at the hospital. The smell of sterile ICU permeated me even in the cafeteria, and I had no appetite while there. It was nice to take a quick break in the comfort of my own home. It occurred to me that at any given time, someone would probably be going through a crisis like the one in which I found myself. I will forever be cognizant of the role I will play in their crisis.

As my crisis unfolded, I watched every breath Mom took, thinking it might be her last. Her heart was mending but the stroke blocked her consciousness. We had a glimmer of hope in the desert of tears. Mother seemed to be aware, even lifting her arm on command. Then the realization of her condition seemed to send her countenance into waves of desperation. I guess that was my most heart-wrenching moment. It was sad to see her lifeless, but it was agonizing to watch her desperation. She lapsed back behind her lifeless veil. I was grateful. Time would tell the extent of the damage.

Time became a double-edged sword during the close of the crisis. Each day brought a new level of desperation. We were on a roller coaster of hope and despair. I longed for shreds of recovery for Mom one minute, then the next I prayed for God to take her. I felt guilty in looking for signs of the end, yet her seemingly empty eyes haunted me. I had no idea what she could understand, and my senses betrayed me. One minute it felt like I connected with her, and the next I only sensed empty reflexes. I felt responsible without any control. I was worn out trying to make the situation better, and I was caught in the murkiness of waiting. My energies and my emotions were spent, yet my sleep was restless. I trusted God implicitly with both her future and mine, but I dreaded the handwriting on the wall. God knew the cry of my heart and hers, and I prayed for strength and courage for all of us to continue.

If Mom recovered, she would face aggressive therapy in an effort to achieve a level of recovery I feared would not be acceptable to her. Good heart, good lungs and functioning kidneys became a detriment in light of the stroke. We would be responsible for putting her through this "last ditch effort" with a broken and weary body and spirit, yet this would be her best shot at any recovery. The doctors had already gone against her wishes by putting a temporary feeding tube in her nose. This supplied her nutritional needs for the moment. Even though it was temporary, we all knew she would be vehemently against it. That decision weighed heavy on all of us, and we could sense the disgust she felt when she reached for her nose. Time seemed to be of the essence to secure our best hopes, and I knew God was abundantly able to perform miracles, yet the odds seemed to be stacked against us. We walked the fine line between hope and despair, and the neurologist insisted that we must be patient. I kept hoping that God would pull us out of this pit but days continued to pass. I strained to see the good God was fashioning, trusting that it existed. I drew on His promise not to forsake us in these seemingly endless dark hours. I knew He would deliver us safely in His own time.

I felt wasted, getting up at 5:30 a.m., arriving at the hospital by 7:00 a.m. and staying all day. I felt guilty leaving around 7:30 p.m. at night. I struggled to leave, knowing I needed to rest up for the same routine the next day. There was so much to coordinate – doctors, therapists, meal attempts, moving to other facilities. Mom could not talk, so someone had to be there to coordinate her progress. I felt like I needed permission to leave or to take a break, but who gives the permission? There were so many changes in her progress. One minute we considered Hospice, and then at the slightest progress, we were headed to aggressive physical, speech and occupational therapy. We often digressed to a nursing home decision. It became amusing to see which coat we wore for the moment and how fast and frequently we changed coats.

It was shocking to hear the word Hospice as one possibility. I knew in my head the good Hospice does, and I have even heard myself talk to others about the benefits of Hospice. But knowing in my head was light years from accepting with my heart. I felt myself drowning in the swell of emotions.

Day after day we rode the wave of hope only to crash into the pit of depression. I saw momentary recognition in Mom's eyes, recognition of her plight. I am not sure, but I know she cried. It was brief then she slipped away. I wished I could slip away. However, my pain would be unbearable if she could not escape. I assured her that her future was safe. If she could get better we would be with her every step of the way, but if she could not, we would let her go. Removing the feeding tube loomed as a dreadful decision. It was going to take some time to determine whether or not she would get better. I was grateful for the doctor's assistant who assured me that they would help us make that determination. More time passed.

After a while, we were faced with having to move Mom from ICU. Fortunately we were able to move her to a private room for a couple of days until we could find another placement. The feeding tube became an issue in the new placement. One facility would only accept Mom if she had a peg tube, a tube inserted directly into the stomach, but another facility would possibly take her with the feeding tube in the nose. Fortunately an aggressive speech therapist hurried a test that determined Mom could swallow. After the test, the therapist sat Mom up and even put a spoon in her left hand. After a little nudge, Mom began to feed herself, even scraping the bottom of the spoon against the bowl to prevent dripping. Not only did she pass the swallowing test, but she even seemed to perk up when we applauded her success. The feeding tube was removed and now Mom's fate seemed to be totally in God's hands, removing any future "hard call" from our shoulders. On the upswing, we moved Mom to a skilled nursing unit for aggressive therapy. As we approached each fork in the road, we found only one way to go. That was a good thing.

Chapter 2

Survival

Mom's surviving the stroke was terrifying for me, and I felt guilty for my feelings. Not only was Mom's life forever altered, but mine was altered as well. My responsibilities were put on hold during the crisis, but I began to realize that I would have to merge my busy life and current everyday tasks with tending to and supporting Mom at a high level. I was overcome with guilt in thinking of myself. Mother was suffering greatly and I was thinking about how it affected me! Then I realized the blessing Mom bestowed on all of us to help us get through this very time. She told us many times that if she were ever dependent and in need of full-time care, she wanted us to put her in a well-equipped nursing home with personnel trained to handle the demands and go on about our business. She made it clear that she did not want family involved in providing daily care and hygiene for her. Although we were not at the nursing home stage yet, replaying her words helped me survive her survival. It did not absolve me of my duties, but it helped me to face the tasks ahead.

A deep sadness settled over the family as this process continued. Mother had suffered the heart attack pains one evening, but the pains subsided so she decided not to tackle the emergency room. At my insistence, she called the doctor the next day and followed his instructions to go to the emergency room. Later, I lamented my insistence because although all of her arteries supplying her heart were critically blocked and there was a 50-50 chance that she would suffer a major heart attack within a week, at this juncture the heart attack seemed to be the lesser of the two evils. I tried to steer away from hindsight entrapment.

Anyway, Mom drove herself to the hospital. For Mom, driving was her badge of independence. It was difficult for us to face the fact that she would never drive again. She would no longer bring me lunch at work or take cookies to someone in need. She would no longer leave a family gathering early to feed her dog or arrive on Christmas morning toting "Nana rolls" and her famous dressing. It was also difficult to walk into her house to see everything suspended for her return. As I walked through her back door, I envisioned her sitting at the kitchen bar reading the paper and drinking coffee. Her glasses were still lying on the bar as she had left them. She would probably never return to live there. Even if she could make some type of recovery, we had lost our independent Mom and the warmth of home as we knew it.

After she moved to the skilled nursing facility, the signs that Mom was improving seem to disintegrate. The thought that she could feed herself in a seemingly cognitive way raised our hopes. One night when presented with a bit of her expensive night cream on her finger, I thought she might be able to apply it to her face. Hopefully, I nudged her finger toward her cheek and to my horror she licked it off her finger. She did not even make a face with the flavor. My heart sank, and as my husband concluded, we may have read into her actions a little too much. She regained her automatic mannerisms: the way she held a spoon, moved her arm, rubbed her eye and adjusted her hair. However she was far from recapturing understanding. My prayer for Mom during this time of confusion and disorientation was that she could see the unseen and that she felt God's presence more clearly. She was lost in a haze, and I did not want her to be alone.

I felt I was operating on God's strength alone. My major task during this stage was to devise a schedule for Mom that met her needs. I felt compelled to be there until she was "fixed." I became the point person responsible for coordinating all of the people involved in her care. My brother, Drew, was the point person for the bills and all of the financial aspects of her care. I was grateful for a partner to shoulder the burden and remember thinking to myself that there should be a law against having "only children." I know the crisis brought us closer. I still had pangs of anguish when I left her side. She was dependent on the care and compassion of the nurses and aides. I asked for God's guardian angels to watch over her. I had always believed in guardian angels for babies and surmised that there must be guardian angels for the helpless regardless of the age. I felt like I existed on borrowed energies. The tears did not come as often and the panic changed to acquiescence.

Then acquiescence flared into exasperation. It felt like God had turned a deaf ear to all of us. I knew my timing was not God's, but the agony continued. One morning Mom was sitting up in bed when I arrived, looking normal and alert. She was holding Drew's hand, and when I approached she lifted her hand for mine. She looked like she was fully cognizant. Later, during physical therapy, she participated; then things started to crumble. She was miserable sitting in the chair, and as the day progressed, she seemed to take a nosedive. She refused to eat lunch, and throughout the afternoon grunted either in pain or anguish with every breath. She seemed so desperate. She ate a few bites for dinner then refused everything else. I begged God to take her home, ending her entrapment. What possible good could come from her lingering like this? There was no progress, only pain. My heart broke again and again and still the heartbreak continued. Surely God knew the cry of our hearts. Why was He silent? Where should we go from here?

As the days passed, I was faced with resuming portions of my routines. I had been in an altered state for so long that my normal activities seemed unfamiliar and empty. Although many around me expressed concern for my plight, they seemed to be able to move from concern back into normal with ease, whereas I was stuck in my emotional emergency. It was hard to maintain composure and to motivate myself to participate in the mundane activities. I think the most disturbing thing for me was to realize that eventually I would slip back into ordinary life as well, forgetting the critical life and death issues with which I had been entwined.

At times I emerged from the depths of loss to see aspects of Mom I had not lost. Although her meticulously groomed outer shell was markedly different, her unsinkable spirit surfaced in me. It seemed like a simple action, but in retrospect I saw the ripple effect of Mom's character. One of Mom's concerns when she was not able to return home from the hospital before the surgery was that she had not made her bed. She said that this was the only time in the last twenty years that she had left the house without making her bed. Although this practice was ingrained in my normal schedule, during the crisis I had failed to make my bed as well. One day I found myself making the bed, and recognizing the root of this habit comforted me. It was a catalyst for contemplating the many facets of Mom's values, the part that would outlive the flesh. She touched so many lives with her wit and emotional fortitude, and at that moment I realized that we would never lose her essence.

At the heart of Mom's fundamental nature was a fighting spirit, and fight she did! We had good days when she sat with dignity in the wheelchair, insisting on feeding herself, and assisted the therapists with standing, sitting, and movement. She surfaced unexpectedly with decided alertness, and (although inconsistently) even responded appropriately with hand gestures. Following these cues we settled into a survival mode with long-term planning. I envisioned spending quality time with her and even made mental notes as to how we could spend that time. Then there were days filled with pain and restless anxiety. Regressing, she would display grimacing expressions alternating with blank looks. I doubted her presence and hoped she was able to escape the imprisonment. At this juncture I prayed for release.

During the fight, Drew and I agonized over Mom's presence of mind. We could not determine the extent to which she was aware of either her own condition or her surroundings. We vacillated on whether or not she knew us or anyone else. In addition, she seemed to come in and out of focus. The idea that she was fully cognizant in a hopelessly unresponsive body plagued us and we wondered what we were doing in putting her through the agony of these futile attempts to recover miniscule and unacceptable function. We were completely clear on her wishes in the event of this type of tragedy and we were tormented by her helpless body enduring the extended pain and loss of dignity. However, the professionals we looked to for guidance continued to indicate that it was too soon to give up.

As the battle for recovery continued, Mom fought a horrific infection in both legs which ultimately required her to endure another surgery to clean out the debris. The surgery took us back to ICU, evoking chilling déjà vu. It was recognizable territory, so it was easier to traverse, but I was surprised how quickly and vigorously my panic returned. Having lost naïve invincibility concerning surgery, I felt extremely vulnerable, knowing how quickly and easily things could go wrong. Although small as it was, Mom had gained some ground so I was reluctant to put her hard-fought progress back into jeopardy. Still ambivalent about the outcome of her recovery, I did not know whether to welcome the crisis as a possible release from this dilemma or dig in to protect the ground we had gained. Once again, we came to a crossroad with only one clear path to take. Because it was too soon to give up, we shuffled timidly ahead.

The second surgery proved successful, and Mom persevered with surprising stamina. She emerged from the stroke stupor in the mornings with ever-increasing alertness and there were more and more times that we knew she was with us. We celebrated her victories much like we did our children's firsts. We kept a notebook in her room to chronicle each day's successes and to convey progress viewed to one another. We became partners with the therapists in trying various communication techniques, and milestones were definitely reached; for example, she was able to answer yes/no questions with hand gestures and by pointing to words written on a white board. Before long we seemed to be communicating on a consistent basis.

For me, communicating with Mom in this stage of survival was a double-edged sword. Communication with her seemed consistent on most simple questions but too problematic on other questions to trust. For the most part, she lacked expression or initiative. Certain responses plagued me. From the time she emerged from the first surgery, she would persistently throw the TV/nurse call button apparatus on the floor in an apparent tantrum. Her reaction to the TV was understandable, but when I tried to show her the nurse's call button, she persisted in discarding the whole thing. She barely tolerated its presence in the vicinity of her bed, despite my explanation of its necessity. This child-like response made me question her understanding and therefore her apparent answers to simple questions. I longed for the assurance that she could get what she needed, and her using the call button would grant me that assurance, yet she refused to comply like a little child. Which reply could I trust, and which reply was unreliable? How I wished I could somehow find out!

Chapter 3

Adaptation

Survival turned in to an adaptation period in which we meshed the new reality with previous normality, an awkward adjustment at best. What had become routine during crisis and survival had to be integrated with previously full schedules. However for me, the practical was much easier to adjust than the mind-set, and managing time was easier than managing emotions. I resumed ordinary responsibilities and carefully maximized my time to include hospital shifts, but I was harnessed with weighty, reflective perspectives. I could not seem to resume a casual approach to my life.

Saturdays were the worst for me. I could lose myself in the busyness of the other days, but Saturdays were typically my day to sleep late, relax, shop, and catch up on personal errands. These "normal" activities eluded me, and so did my composure. The reality was that both Mom's and my life had forever changed and there was nothing I could do about it. I could not escape the enormity of the change, nor could I pull myself out of the resulting depression. What was kept at bay by the distractions of my job engulfed me during down times. The times that had previously recharged me now served as a forum for intense contemplation. I had difficulty dealing with trivial pursuits and felt alone on this reflective track.

There were moments of clarity along this philosophical path--priceless epiphanies that forced unexpected growth. All my life I had struggled for Mom's approval, and although she expressed her admiration of me to others, I rarely received that validation directly from her. She supported me with her actions, not her words. Now I was in the position of making decisions for her, and with her lack of expression and unreliable communication skills, there was no way for me to gain her endorsement for the decisions I was making. The positive strokes I longed for were locked away, and I had to find a way to authenticate what I was doing on my own.

One day I had bought some clothes for her to use in her therapy. She needed sweatpants (which she did not own), so I went all over town collecting possible options for her. I struggled to get them all up to the hospital room in one trip but I succeeded. Once there, I began to seek her approval. I held the first one up and she shook her head emphatically, "No." Then I held up the next option and got the same response. My heart began to sink as I was going through the pile. There were no other options in town. What would I do if she refused all of them? I lingered over some of the options that seemed the best to me, and she still shook her head, "NO." Sure enough, she refused all of them. I was in tears as I hauled the pile back to my car. I sat there for a few minutes in utter exhaustion and exasperation. I was faced with providing a pair of sweatpants the next day and Mom had just refused the entirety of the supply I had at my disposal. Plus, I had to return all of those clothes to the various stores. I sat there in the car desperately praying for a solution.

How quickly I had slipped back into acquiescent childhood behavioral patterns. After a full day of shopping for Mom and another afternoon showing her the selections, I was sitting in the car in tearful frustration at not pleasing her as I had done so many times in my childhood. It occurred to me that even now in her presence, I instinctively fell into dependent thinking, and I caught myself in the midst of the irony. It really didn't matter which pair of sweatpants I chose, but I needed to be the one to choose one. Mom had to have a pair by tomorrow, and I would be the one who selected it. Mom did not have to approve. I must make the decisions now for her and feel good about it.

All of a sudden I realized that I was thrust into the power position and conversely the look on Mom's face when I left her resembled the innocence of a child. I felt like Dorothy in the Wizard of Oz when she discovered that the power to return home was within her all along. Not only did I possess the inner strength to confirm my own decisions, but Mom was dependent on my ability to do that very thing. Nevertheless, this change in my perception of the relationship would definitely require some time and careful consideration.

I began to reflect on the aspects of my relationship with Mom and, in turn, the aspects of my relationship with my children. Control and acceptance had shifted in my relationship with Mom, and although this had arguably happened over time, it was never discussed. I realized that we had operated instinctively in the relationship and had not redefined our relationship as it evolved. I had lamented the fact that I did not have the pleasure of an adult relationship with my father because he was snatched from us in an airplane crash just after I graduated from college. Now I realized that I had not recognized and celebrated my independence and was just now taking ownership of the acceptance issues. I am sure Mom did acknowledge my growth, and I know she was proud of the woman I had become, but by not openly discussing it, I missed the blessing bestowed and subconsciously operated in a reduced capacity in her presence. I did not want to miss conferring the blessing on my children openly and joyously.

The adaptation of mind-set continued to evolve as the weeks passed and I continued to make decisions for Mom without seeking her approval. She also made remarkable improvement. We began answering inquiries with guarded optimism and found ourselves relaying information about Mom's progress instead of her decline. She began to communicate yes and no answers by shaking her head. Her alertness became dependable and her legs began to heal. There was progression in her ability to stand for short periods, and she even helped propel herself in the wheelchair with her good leg and arm. I tried not to think of the future and focused on the successes of the day because, although she had made great strides, there was still a very long way to go.

God's grace became my mainstay, and if I remained in the moment I could keep my balance. There was no end in sight, and I had to settle into the role of primary caregiver. If I could just do what I could at the moment, I seemed to be able to keep equilibrium among all of my responsibilities. I hung on to a phrase I had learned during previous trying times: "Grace for the moment." It proved reliable in developing the mental muscle to bear the burden I had unwittingly found on my shoulders. My emotional emergency shifted from losing my Mom to losing my independence.

I began to work through the ways in which I had been tethered to Mom both emotionally and now physically. Before her stroke I was stuck in a pattern of seeking verbal approval from her. Although it was sometimes a source of amusement to me to see the ways in which Mom would disapprove of my hair, dress, actions, or purchases, I subconsciously held on to the expectation that someday I would achieve a level of sanction. The recognition of that bondage and the realization that Mom would probably no longer be able to grant my need for her authorization broke that emotional string for me. My "Wizard of Oz" moment when I realized I had the power all along freed me and allowed me to put away the constraint in our connection I had harbored since childhood only to replace it with a different attachment.

Now it was her need that I was fulfilling, a reversal of roles I found unsettling not because of the tasks at hand, but because I lost the one person in the world whose perceived job was to unconditionally take care of me. She was faithful in that aspect of her role, and even though I had outgrown the need for that type of attention, I had the security of the relationship. Her ability to fulfill her position of mother as I had known it was forever altered, and I was deeply grieved. I was glad to provide for Mom in ways I had not had the opportunity to serve my dad. The challenge was to grant myself permission to do all I could do for her and still carry on with my life without regretting the manner in which I balanced both.

In the succeeding weeks, I had to remind myself repeatedly that I could only do what I could do at the moment and that was enough. I treasured the friends who helped me justify preserving my sanity and who came to rescue me from my own conscientiousness. Permission was a treasured commodity. I made a mental note to help others validate themselves during similar role reversals. I allowed myself momentary diversions of thought and took 10 minute vacations from the tasks that seemed to pile up in all aspects of my life. It was easy to be overwhelmed, but for the most part, I was uplifted and sustained by an army of anonymous prayer warriors I am convinced were working on my behalf. There was no other explanation for the peace in my heart.

Chapter 4

Depression

Although functioning in this new reality, I found myself in the midst of a cloud of depression. Mom continued to make gradual progress, and I was elated with each accomplishment. However, the momentum in my life was at a standstill, and I could not shake caregiver's melancholy. It was sticky and repressive, and I felt guilty for my self-centered frame of mind. After all, Mom was experiencing the real trauma, so why should I be in a slump? It was as if I could not take a deep breath until she was released, and all I wanted to do was escape. We seemed to be tethered to what I perceived to be the same stifling air supply and I felt claustrophobic. At times she was in better spirits than I was, determined to clear hurdles and exhausted by the end of each day. I moved about my daily activities with the enthusiasm of a robot and an unshakable apathy. All I wanted to do was escape so I used food, sleep and mindless game playing on the computer to distract me. I felt alone in my fog, too ashamed to admit my self-absorption.

My prison was more emotional than physical. My chores were not inordinate; it was the confinement of my mind during my "free time." I managed to surround my visits with Mom by healthy boundaries, but it was the constant burden of responsibility that tethered my life-force. Her meals could be ordered in the rehab facility within minutes, and her laundry could be done quickly and efficiently, but it was the regularity of these tasks and the uncertainty of the duration that weighed heavily on my spirit. The yoke of disability left little promise for my future freedom, and I had to reckon with this unwelcomed halter. My load was very light in comparison to that of others, and I reminded myself regularly that my burdens must make me better not bitter. However, it felt like my life was standing still while others went about theirs.

While my life was on hold, Mom made remarkable progress in many respects. Her stamina and strength increased as the infection in her legs subsided. She began to help the aides with transferring from the bed to the wheelchair, was able to sit for extended periods of time, and persistently participated in all aspects of her rehabilitation. She began to experience slight movement in her affected leg and worked tirelessly to stand and walk.

Mentally, Mom seemed to be cognizant most of the time and was consistently able to nod and shake her head appropriately in response to questions. With prompting, she even began to repeat simple words. Because communication is a complicated system of processing both input and output, and someone experiencing difficulty in producing output typically experiences a corresponding difficulty in processing input, her understanding was still somewhat suspect. However, we were certain she understood most of what was going on even though she rarely initiated verbal responses without reminders.

I was still plagued with her response to the nurses' call button. She still refused to have anything to do with it, much less use it. At one juncture I believe we were refused admittance to a nursing facility because of her inability use the call button to signal assistance. I lectured her many times on the importance of her demonstrating her ability to call for help so she grudgingly allowed the apparatus on her bed. However, she persisted in placing it near the edge of the bed or under the covers with a childish defiant glare. Despite her amazing progress, without the assurance that she could illicit help when she needed it, I continued to feel the confinement of her disability, locked in the resulting inertia of despair.

In her ineluctable way, Mom rescued me from persistent doldrums. Because she did not initiate speech but only mimicked words, we had to find a way to communicate nonverbally. Mom had always exhibited a stoic demeanor and was not by nature demonstrative, so we traversed new ground with lingering eye contact, enduring hugs, and facial caresses. It was fun for me to initiate these encounters, and although she had always been an unwilling captive, she responded tenderly. I soaked up every precious moment thinking each might have to suffice. In trying to focus not only on memorizing the moments but discerning Mom's needs, I began to connect to her spirit. Even though she had few facial expressions, her eyes were expressive and they conveyed her thoughts unmistakably.

Certain looks triggered a replay of previous conversations to the point that I began hearing her voice. As she said over and over in the past, I could once again hear her say, "Go on and do what you need to do. You had better get to gettin'." Her independence permeated her unresponsive body and proved to be the catalyst for me to begin the ascent out of the very real and valid depression that most certainly overtakes all involved in such tragedy. I made a mental note to bless my kids with similar conversations to replay if needed.

Ascent out of depression was on a slippery slope. We would make progress then slide back into the mire. Throughout the ordeal Mom had displayed surprisingly good spirits, and I was amazed at the consistency with which she would almost cheerfully wave goodbye when I left. In my mind I rationalized that the depression medication Mom was on coupled with her suspect ability to process input produced this positive disposition. Or could this be another selfless, motherly gift to me?

We had to move Mom from the rehab floor of the hospital to a skilled nursing home facility for further therapy. I transported her in my car and noticed a different demeanor as we approached the facility. Putting my best, most optimistic spin on the move, I assured Mom that we were still seeking the most aggressive therapy plan we could provide and this nursing home was best facility in town to receive that therapy. She took it like a trooper, but I felt the sadness thickening in the car, overtaking both of us. When faced with adversity, Mom would historically display a tough, unsinkable spirit with something like, "We'll just have to hump up and do it." However, in this moment her eyes betrayed her, and I caught a glimpse of her vulnerable, emotional side. Still, she was able to conceal her emotions from me for a few more days.

Optimism and sadness rotated through the revolving door of these days. We shared some absolutely priceless times. I looked forward to relishing each moment with her and made plans in my mind for future occasions. We joined hands and spirits in focused and extended prayer. We hugged each other with a grasp that united our innermost beings. We laughed until tears rolled down our cheeks when despite all of her efforts and intentions the only word she could muster was pastrami. Then one afternoon I came face to face with the crashing realization that Mom was fully cognizant of her situation, placing her in the middle of her worst nightmare and me in the helpless position of watching it unfold. After a precious time of praying together and contemplating hearing God's voice, I turned to her and asked her if she liked it in the facility. The mask of courage she was maintaining seemingly for my benefit melted before my eyes as she sighed and revealed deep sorrow in the depths of her eyes. She tried to look away to hide her despair but it overwhelmed her. Neither of us could contain the tears anymore as we held each other in hopelessness. Why did God ignore the cry of our hearts?

Drew confirmed Mom's extended depressed state. We compared notes, and he caught glimpses of the same sadness Mom revealed to me. Somehow, it was comforting to share our respective grief and ponder the alternatives even though nothing could be resolved. Her future would be determined by the progress she could make, and it was out of our control. Walking out the door leaving her sitting in her wheelchair alone was indeed the hardest thing we had to face, and we faced it regularly. I did not think my heart could break any more, and I prayed for the calluses to grow quickly. Every time I left with tears in my eyes and an ache in my heart, as did my brother.

In the ensuing days, I began to appreciate the advantages of Mom's stoic nature. I welcomed it when it surfaced in place of obvious hopelessness. On many occasions I rounded the corner into her room to see her contentedly watching TV. She would perk up and wave with a half-smile, greeting me with a warm left-handed hug. Then she would try to speak, but after a few minutes of struggling, she would sigh and resort to a meaningful nod. I marveled at her composed display of grit. Her mask of courage made visiting easier for me.

During her stay in skilled nursing, Mom's infections cleared, she regained some movement in her right leg, and she was able to mimic short sentences when prompted. That was good enough for me. One Sunday

I coaxed her into attending a short church service at the nursing home and to my amazement discovered that she could sing. Apparently that part of her rote memory was intact, and she really had no difficulty singing songs she knew from the past. "Happy Birthday" was her best song, so we capitalized on it at future family birthday parties.

My visits became more routine and centered on helping her with daily hygiene. I helped her with brushing her teeth, cleaning her face, and applying lotion. I still grappled with Mom's behavioral inconsistencies resulting from her stroke. At times her behavior prompted our assumption that she was fully cognizant but locked in an unresponsive body. However, at other times key connections were obviously missing. I took her some of her makeup and arranged one-handed access, but it was apparent she did not know the function of some of the items I brought. She applied her perfume spray as hand lotion and seemed confused when I corrected her. Once again my assumptions proved inaccurate so I adjusted my expectations.

After returning home from the perfume incident steeped with Mom's scent on my hands, our dog, Lucy, began squealing and searching the house for her beloved Nana. Lucy's reaction triggered the memories of Mom walking through my front door and sadly, I shared the flashback with Lucy. I missed so many aspects of our previous relationship that could not be recouped: the regular phone calls, her answers to cooking questions, having lunch with her, stopping by her house for a quick visit, her candid reactions, to name only a few. Much of Mom's essence was gone even though she lingered. I savored the memories as the scent faded.

Chapter 5

Custodial Care

In the ensuing months, Mom moved from skilled nursing to custodial care at the nursing home with the promise that she would still receive a level of restorative care. The aides would continue to try to walk her when time permitted. This continued level of therapy justified her stay at this nursing home facility and helped us wade through the looming, long-term reality of her situation. This arrangement was still temporary in our minds. However, the financial burden of maintaining her empty home forced us to into long-term thinking. The task was to create a new home for mom, not merely to juggle the logistics of her care. Breaking up her home meant more to me that just selling her house; it was a metamorphosis I hadn't anticipated.

No matter how hard I tried, I couldn't picture the nursing home as Mom's new home, although the facility was very nice. We brought pictures to her room, and although we were allowed to bring some of her furniture, we never did. As someone put it, "People go to the nursing home to get well and go home, or they get worse and die. In any case, it is a temporary place." That seemed to epitomize my feelings. Restlessly, I struggled to explore any option, no matter how remote.

For me, the days in the nursing home were characterized by an ache in the pit of my stomach. I was okay when I arrived, but leaving was extremely difficult, and I had a hard time walking out and leaving Mom there alone. Although it was better than the hospital, it still felt like an institution, not a home. Her care seemed adequate but the environment was emotionally sterile. The lobby was pleasantly decorated with colorful birds in cages, a water fountain, and seasonal decorations. I couldn't help but draw a somewhat warped analogy between the colorful birds in cages and colorful personalities in similar cages.

Most days I was greeted in the lobby by the usual group. There was a gentleman in a baseball cap tethered to his wheelchair with an alarm. He was noted for trying to escape through the front door. He had one arm in a sling and although he did not speak, he always smiled and waved with his good arm. He had a wonderful twinkle in his eye. There was a lady who wandered aimlessly in the halls in her wheelchair. She would beckon anyone near with a "Come here darlin', please, please." When you responded, she looked puzzled as to your intentions. Many times she would be stuck facing the wall, unable to maneuver like a wind-up car, spinning its wheels in a corner. The staff seemed to be immune to her pleas, as was I, after a surprisingly short time. There was usually a group of ladies at a table, some verbal, some not. Each would smile as I made eye contact. One lady would always greet me with an enthusiastic wave. Although she had difficulty speaking, I knew she was really glad to connect. Mom never joined the lobby bunch. She just didn't seem to fit in.

Mom stayed on the skilled nursing wing in the nursing home even after her skilled nursing days ran out because the bathroom configuration of her room was suited to her needs. It was good that she did not have to move, but it kept her among the most transient residents. One lady under hospice care was out of her mind. She would consistently call out, "Help me, help me! I'm cold and I need some cover! I need some cover!" Many times I would hear a nurse assure her that she had cover and she needed to calm down as to not disturb the other residents. Although she was extremely frail and unable to comprehend her situation, her constant pleas had a noticeable effect on her neighbors.

Mom managed to make some friends. However, most of her friends were able to move on after a time. I visited with two special friends who ate at Mom's table. They were particularly endearing to me because they looked out for Mom and would fill me in on things that would happen. They recounted the Halloween party, informed me when Mom joined them for bingo, and kept me posted on Mom's appetite and spirits. I had mixed emotions when one of them left to go home. Of course I was glad for her progress, but I selfishly missed her support.

Mom's room in the nursing home consisted of a bed, dresser with TV on top, night stand, a couple of chairs, and two tables. Because she had been a card player, we moved a computer into the room on which she occasionally played solitaire. Through working with the mouse, her coordination with her left hand improved. I struggled to think of activities for her. She indicated that she couldn't read so I brought her books on tape, which she enjoyed.

In addition to the books on tapes, I brought a number of puzzles with large pieces. She enjoyed sitting by me as I worked the puzzle, and occasionally she was able to join in when I placed a piece in her hand and nudged her in the right direction. She still seemed to have a processing problem, and even when I placed the piece in her hand with the correct orientation, she still had to work to get it to fit. However mysteriously, it wouldn't take long for the puzzles to be completed. I asked Mom if she was working the puzzles in my absence and she would laugh and shrug her shoulder. The mystery was solved one day when I rounded the corner to find this one particular aide busily huddled over the puzzle. This aide was the "slow" aide, and I suspected she had a touch of mental retardation. However, she was sweet to Mom. "I have to come in and help her out with the puzzle," she said proudly. Mom and I laughed when she left. I was happy to supply the aide with puzzles. It provided company of sorts for Mom.

One day the nursing home staff found Mom on

the floor. They rushed her to the emergency room for X-rays even though she didn't seem to be hurt. She was bruised but had no broken bones. However, the facility had a zero tolerance policy with this type of event. I had to do some fast talking to keep Mom out of a restraining device to keep her seated in her wheelchair. I rationalized to the staff that I had seen Mom slumped over in her wheelchair several times, fast asleep. This was a sight that was indelibly burned in my memory and still brings tears to my eyes. Grasping, I assured the staff that she had fallen asleep and tumbled out of her wheelchair. Reluctantly they agreed to give her another chance without restraints.

Mom still refused to employ the call button. She rolled herself out into the hall and waved someone down when she needed something. I continued to lecture her about calling someone when she needed to lie down, to which she shrugged. She was found on the floor two more times and I guess my non-threatening attitude towards each event kept her from being restrained. In a precautionary move, I changed her routine and asked the staff to lay her down after lunch. This seemed to help.

The sage advice of a life-long friend echoed in my mind. In retrospect after losing both of her parents, she encouraged me to orchestrate the precious time remaining with my Mom with meaningful moments. She recommended interspersing opportunities to serve Mom with rich reminiscence, plenty of hugs, and a hearty dose of laughter. I began to plan my time with Mom and searched for ways to share spiritual perspectives. I had led many prayers with Mom, and during each she participated with consistent fervor. However, I felt the need to delve deeper into a spiritual connection. We did not have a history of sharing spiritual things except on a cursory level, so I searched prayerfully for a venue. Through divine provision we embarked on a quest to hear God's voice through reading a Joy Dawson book together, *Forever Ruined for the Ordinary: The Adventure of Hearing and Obeying God's Voice*. I began reading the book to her months earlier, but I started over and felt led to "discuss" it with her. The paradox of discussing a book with someone who has lost the ability to speak still amuses me, but discuss we did.

Mom engaged in the discussions with rich facial expressions. I became adept at reading her expressions and vocalizing them as they appeared. Prior to the tragedy I made little eye contact with her, perhaps in an effort to dodge anticipated disapproval. Once I abandoned my quest for sanction, I was able to see past my childhood perception of Mom. Our relationship deepened as we connected in a pure, honest way without the false impressions that words sometimes produce. Her silence removed the judgment barrier of the tongue and I saw her heart through the window of her eyes. I felt her love through meaningful touch and the message was unmistakable. We shared an abiding mutual respect through this nonverbal language.

In addition to the nonverbal expressions, I was able to tell her how much I admired her, and she was able to hear me without brushing off my comments with her self-conscious air. I bathed her in positive comments about her talents, sacrifices, and tenacity. We reminisced and I took the opportunity to verbalize my appreciation for the things she provided throughout my lifetime.

We also shared precious spiritual time. One day, we joined hands to pray and I asked her to start the prayer. She did. Although it was inaudible, I felt her pour out her heart. I made it a point from then on to allow her time to speak.

Our discussions began to reveal the women in both of us, and I was surprised at the commonalities and the twists in roles. I began to see her strength in myself and my vulnerabilities in her face. I became her cheerleader whereas she had always been my number one fan. Her grit surfaced in my determination for her to improve, and I found her words coming out of my mouth, "We'll just have to hump up and do this together." I exerted a dominating presence as she took on the quiet spirit. I understood her contemplative looks because I spent my childhood lost in thought. I led the charge in questioning procedures and protocols as she settled into acceptance. We both emerged amalgamated, tempered with each other's traits. We retained our individuality but the family resemblance was striking. For so many years I had fought our differences only to wind up uncovering our similarities.

One distinguishing trait to which we both persistently adhered was a fiercely independent nature. Both of us tended to shut others out, relying on ourselves for the answers. Our study in the Dawson book revealed the fallacy of this independent state, the sin of audacious self-reliance. That in which we had previously invested pride was now an impediment to overcome. Humility was the first condition of hearing God's voice, and although it was not hard to be humble with respect to our individual accomplishments, it was extremely difficult to shed our self-sufficiency.

Mom had lost her mother when she was twelve years old, so I presume her autonomy was developed through the absence of motherly encouragement. She lived with her aunt and became responsible for most of the cooking for that family at a very early age. I can only imagine what it must have been like for her, but I assume she learned to wear her capabilities as armor, protecting her vulnerability. Like many others experiencing their childhood during the Great Depression, physical needs overshadowed the emotional, so that generation tended to develop exceptional resourcefulness with an accompanying stoicism.

Mom became an entrepreneur in high school, servicing vending machines for spending money. Without a model for patterning emotional support, she excelled in providing for her children the basics she lacked in her childhood. She tirelessly and selflessly cooked, cleaned, and sewed for her children and sacrificed personal amenities to provide them for us. I truly believe she would have provided the supportive words for which I longed had she known how. How could she give what she never received? She came from a generation of parents who would have sacrificed anything for their children. I slowly began to understand and appreciate her heritage.

My independent state was just as deeply rooted. Through my unconscious and unanswered quest for approval, I developed calluses around my disappointment and aloofly shut others out as a protection mechanism. I retreated to my own world and immersed myself in dreams, awaiting my white knight. This set me up for a life of unfulfilled expectations. My pursuit of Mom's illusive support kept me unconsciously distant in casual relationships but perilously vulnerable to those who held significance in my life. Those special relationships, those whom I let into my inner circle, unbeknownst to them, would have unhealthy power to wound me. Both Mom and I had developed strong defenses stemming from a lack of emotional nurturing. Mom developed a confrontational façade, avoiding feeling weak or dependent, and I acquiesced, withdrawing to avoid feeling empty. We both needed to be liberated from self-reliance, and Mom's tragedy was the catalyst.

As we studied the conditions of hearing God's voice in *Forever Ruined for the Ordinary*, we got stuck at the beginning on the faith condition in which we must trust that God has the answers and that His plans for us are good. We had a hard time accepting this plan because it was definitely not what either of us would choose. Of course it was easier for me, but Mom was angry and had a hard time praying on her own. She was eager to pray when I initiated and was open to praying with others as well. However, when I asked her if she prayed on her own, she consistently shook her head no. I struggled to find ways to help her deal with the anger. I longed for her to be able to hear God's voice and shed her defenses, letting peace reside in place of stoic resistance.

Another condition of hearing God's voice we encountered was yielded will, giving both of us an opportunity to practice vulnerability by surrendering control. While Mom was an unwilling captive to this condition, I was still a caregiver, having to walk the thin line between advocating for her healing and accepting her fate. It was a balancing act between searching for continued therapy and helping her cope with the inevitability of her condition. The boundaries continued to be fuzzy and both my brother and I debated the wisdom of pushing progress or encouraging decline.

Then by the grace of God, "pay it forward" paid off for Mom. She had extended a kindness to Jerry, a young boy whose mother had died of cancer. For a year and a half Jerry rode his bicycle to our house and Mom fed him breakfast before school. She also packed his lunch and he went to school with Drew. After school Jerry and Drew would come home to our house. Jerry never forgot the kindness during his crisis and now, forty years later, he would be in a position to influence Mom's future during her crisis. Jerry had many business dealings with the owners of a small assisted living facility, and over the years Jerry made it clear how he revered my mother. Because Mom was important to Jerry and he was an important client, the owners went out of their way to provide what Mom needed. What resulted was a chain reaction of events that proved to be nothing less than a miracle.

The events commenced when the owners of the facility recommended Audrey, an occupational therapist, who volunteered to evaluate Mom to see if she would be able to qualify for assisted living. The hurdle Mom would have to clear to qualify was to be able to exit the building unassisted in the event of a fire drill within 13 minutes. This seemed quite impossible at the time, but Audrey turned out to be an angel of hope, uncovering Mom's potential instead of focusing on the limitations of her disability. It was clear that Audrey engaged daily in her mission instead of merely fulfilling the responsibilities of her job.

Audrey recommended an ambitious plan to employ Marilyn, a trusted, able-bodied aide who would work with Mom on a consistent basis to build her strength. Marilyn would capitalize on minor movements Mom could make in her right leg, building up her strength in incremental steps. With proper technique, Audrey was certain Mom would succeed. My spirits lifted for the first time in many months. Trusting in Audrey's assessment, we embarked on what seemed at the time to be mission impossible. Could it be that we would be able to move her out of the nursing home into a beautiful facility that afforded residents a small apartment, excellent food, and more personalized care? Could we finally provide an acceptable permanent solution, a new home? Mom seemed rejuvenated with the challenge.

Still, there were so many obstacles to clear. Not only was the bathroom in the vacant apartment not wheelchair accessible, but the configuration of the toilet was not appropriate for Mom. Would the owners of the facility be amenable to remodeling? The dining area was upstairs and the elevator was very small. Would the caregivers be willing to assist Mom upstairs? What about incontinence care? Assisted living traditionally does not include incontinence care. Could we make additional arrangements? Would the staff at the facility schedule the extra care Mom would need? Would Mom really be able to vacate the building on her own in case of fire? The remarkable answer to all of these questions was yes.

Chapter 6

A New Home

With consistent encouragement from Marilyn, coupled with extraordinary tenacity from both Mom and Marilyn, Mom gained strength in her right leg. I'll never forget my elation when I arrived at the nursing home to witness Mom rising from her bed on her own into a sitting position. Marilyn was just out of reach, coaxing with the tone of a drill sergeant. Marilyn made a minor adjustment in Mom's foot placement as she sat then backed away. "You can do it Mrs. Darby! You can do it," she cheered. Mom stood up, bracing with herself with left arm. Her right arm hung in a sling and she carefully balanced her weight on both legs. She struggled to shift her weight. "Put your weight on your right side, Mrs. Darby. You can do it," Marilyn coached. Mom paused, struggling with both the mental and physical barriers to transferring her weight. With a sudden break in inertia, Mom succeeded, positioning herself in front of her wheelchair. "Lower yourself down, Mrs. Darby.

Don't plop down," instructed Marilyn. Mom carefully grabbed the arm of the wheelchair with her left hand and lowered herself with a somewhat controlled fall. "Come on Mrs. Darby. Use both feet to pull," Marilyn continued. Mom took a moment to catch her breath. Sweat was pouring off both of them as Marilyn glanced down at her watch. "Both feet, Mrs. Darby, pull with both feet. Use that right foot," she urged.

With a major battle under her belt, Mom began moving toward the door of her room. I was timidly peeking into the room holding my breath in anticipation. I had stopped at the door and was watching from afar as if my presence would slow Mom's progress. Red-faced, she picked up momentum and skillfully took the turn from her room into the hall. Marilyn led the way, backing down the hall cheering Mom the whole way. Tears swelled in my eyes as I rooted for the team. I couldn't believe it. The whole process clocked in at just under four minutes. With only a minor adjustment in foot placement, Mom passed the test with flying colors. I was speechless.

With this remarkable progress, we proceeded with the necessary arrangements to move Mom to the apartment in the assisted living facility. They graciously agreed to let us remodel the bathroom and in doing so, remodeled our lives. The apartment consisted of a bedroom, a bathroom, and a living room with a small sink, refrigerator, and a microwave in the entrance area. We moved some of her furniture into it and proceeded to make this her new home. The atmosphere was homey, the food was good, and the caregivers were sensitive. Drew and I both seemed to relax and settle in to a more peaceful state.

Mom seemed happier even though she still struggled with apathy and depression. We searched for activities and encouraged outings. Mom agreed to coming to Drew's home or to mine but rarely joined us in public places. Since she refused to go anywhere, we worked hard to improve her surroundings. We purchased a lift chair that reclined, which afforded her an alternative to sitting in the wheelchair all day. I was puzzled when she didn't seem to like it. We laughed heartily when I made her repeat after me, "I like my lift chair, I like my lift chair, I like my lift chair."

Shortly after we moved, a larger room next door became available. One Saturday after enjoying lunch with Mom, Drew and I took her into the vacant room and casually asked if she would like to move into it. To our dismay she enthusiastically nodded her head. After much discussion, Drew and I concluded that since her room was her entire world, if it would make her happy, we would make the move. Although this room was not wheelchair accessible, we embarked on remodeling it as well.

One day I asked Mom if there was anything from her house that she would like to move into the new room. To my surprise she nodded yes. I started naming over items, and when I came to a sofa, she excitedly nodded yes. Then it dawned on me that she had routinely laid down on her sofa to watch TV. It wasn't that she didn't like her lift chair, it was that she preferred lying down. In her current apartment there was no room for a sofa, but hopefully there would be room in the new apartment. After much negotiation and another bathroom remodel, we successfully moved Mom into her new room, equipping it with a sofa. Immediately she enjoyed sitting and lying on it.

With the move to the new facility, we revisited her health status. We found and treated a squamous cell carcinoma on her ear and had plans to remove another suspicious spot in the same area. Because the facility needed some forms filled out by her physician, I made an appointment with her physician for a checkup. I wasn't sure what questions to ask the physician and how to monitor her various conditions. Her heart was working fine and her blood pressure was better than it had ever been. Because she had a history of other cancers, melanoma, colon cancer, and cancer of the parotid gland, I was unsure about how to proceed with her care. Should we continue with preventative tests such as a regular colonoscopy? Her brother and sister both died from cancer, so the inevitability loomed in the background. I consulted with Drew and we discussed what we would do if we found evidence of cancer. Would we put her through chemotherapy, radiation, or aggressive treatments? We still had the Do Not Resuscitate (DNR) directive in effect. What would we do now? The hard questions continued to surface.

Although we dreaded it, Drew and I decided to have a family discussion to give Mom control of her health care. Drew took the lead in the conversation and reassured her that she was perfectly capable of making decisions for herself. I was in charge of watching her body language to try to verbalize for her. Her expressions turned melancholy and hopeless. We all fought the tears. Finally I turned to her and said, "Do you want to just fix what is broken?" She paused then nodded decidedly. Later, during her appointment, the doctor seemed to assume as much, and we made it through another milestone, somewhat more somber.

Approaching the year mark, we had made each decision to the best of our ability, maintaining a "one day at a time" mentality, taking small steps. Finances dictated selling Mom's home to mobilize her assets. I appreciated my brother's strength during this phase. Neither of us could dwell in the emotional sink hole of memories, so we sifted through her things in short bursts. We opted for outside support to organize an estate sale and boxed up personal mementos to sort through at a later date.

The estate sale proved to be a time of heightened sensitivity for me. Selling Mom's home of forty-seven years meant unearthing memories from the time I was nine years old. A typical Great Depression survivor, Mom never threw anything away. "You might need that someday," was her typical justification. She lived on the edges and top layers of her home. Buried below was rich family history. We were fortunate to employ a very kind and gentle couple, Karen and John, who had been friends for years, to handle the sale. They not only sifted through our family treasures, but appreciated our family heritage. Karen said many times, "You must have had a great childhood." She set aside intimate, personal items and treated them with respect and dignity. I'm not sure I would have made it through the dismantling without her tender attitude.

Because Mom had simple, thrifty taste, her home had become a repository for all of the things Drew and I left behind. Drew left fewer things that I did. He had the usual boyhood items such as Boy Scout memorabilia and football pictures, but I guess boys typically don't save as much as do girls. However, under the layers of possessions lay my own personal museum. Of course Mom saved a number of my baby clothes, shoes, dolls, and doll furniture. Karen was tickled to find my Brownie beanie and assured me that someone would be interested in it. I had a Barbie collection with doll clothes Mom had meticulously made. I stopped in my tracks when I saw my red record player displayed in its glory. The clown still smiled brightly on the inside of the top cover, and the turn table still played on three speeds, 33, 45, and 78. My portable hair dryer with the hose and orange and yellow plastic cap brought memories of dozing while drying my hair. I was surprised that anyone would consider buying my jewelry box with the bent ballerina. I considered taking home each item but remembered they were still at Mom's house because there didn't seem to be a place for them in my home.

I was surprised to note the extent to which Mom's home was an amalgamation of both her experiences and mine. Every time I tried to dispose of items through the

A New Home

years, she would say, "I'll take that. You can't throw that away." She had my dishes complete with stemware from my first marriage. They were newer than her dishes and she needed a change. Prints I brought back from various museums in Europe fit in her home when I wanted to discard them. She carted home most of my children's toys from my garage sales. Both my children and Drew's played vigorously with the toys at Nana's even after they outgrew them in their own home. The discarded toys took on a newfound interest when the cousins gathered at Nana's. Nana never fussed at the mess the kids would make as she stuffed them haphazardly in a cabinet after they left. She allowed the mess but arguing was not tolerated. The important thing was that the cousins became close in the haven she nurtured.

  I was grateful when the estate sale was behind me. When it was over and everything was cleaned out, I walked into the house from the back door for one last look. As I rounded the corner from the utility room into the empty den I was surprised by feelings of déjà vu from the first time I saw the house as a child. I remembered coming into the house and marveling how large the den looked to me then. Oh, how I loved the tile floor from my daddy's tile company! It was comprised of tiny variegated squares. Rugs and furniture had covered that floor for so many years, but now it was revealed as it was the first time I saw it. I gasped as I experienced the excitement I felt then and the anticipation of moving into our new home. I paused to relish the memories. For a moment, I was nine years old again, dancing across that floor, full of unencumbered elation.

As suddenly as the memories descended, they began to fast forward through the years to the screeching realization that perhaps this was the last time I would round that corner to stand in this beloved spot. We already had a contract on the house from an investor who would likely tear out my cherished but outdated tile floor. Soon, everything would be remodeled and what was ending for me would become someone else's beginning. I knew it was as it should be, but it was still an excruciating catharsis.

Chapter 7

Acceptance

I had to let go: let go of Mom's stuff, my stuff, and my attachment to the house. We needed to pool Mom's assets to take care of her, and that gave me strength to let go of the stuff. I held on to the memories but let go of the burden of possessions. I had already let go of my quest for approval from Mom and of the ruts in our relationship. I began to feel lighter, more able to detect the joy hiding in simple moments. I slowed down to enjoy the richness of Mom stroking my face with her hand and, more importantly, stroking my heart with her gaze. I routinely asked her if she needed anything or if I needed to change anything for her, to which she usually shrugged. Instead of rushing to the next service task, I lingered to hold and study her hand, savoring her grip and her admiration. In sensing and enjoying her esteem I was launched into freedom, freedom to be me. Through her eyes and her touch, I began to accept and appreciate my talents.

In releasing belongings, I also loosened my grip

on Mom's situation. It took my ultimate strength to let go, but acceptance brought liberty. Once again, I was struck by the symmetry of opposites; the gain in release. In my single minded quest for verbal approval, I missed the message that was loud and clear. Now through Mom's inability to verbalize, I began to hear her affirmation. The message was unmistakable; I heard it in every encounter: through touch, through looks, and through an inner voice. But before I could hear that inner voice, I had to be to free to accept the message. I had to release my hold on insecurity and appreciate my gifts. I had to discharge meekness to recognize my strengths. By giving myself permission to be grateful for my gifts, I was finally equipped to decipher the steady stream of confirmation not only that Mom was sending, but others were sending as well.

Mom and I continued to share spiritual things. I read to her and she listened intently. I felt her participating. Sadly, Mom continued to be unable to pray, and I struggled for ways to help her with the communication block. At this point I continued to probe into the reasons for her inability to pray. I asked her if she felt close to God to which she shook her head no. "Have you accepted Jesus as your savior?" I asked. The answer was yes. Then I asked if the distant feeling existed before her stroke, and she answered affirmatively. I guess she had believed that Jesus was the Son of God and accepted Him as her savior in baptism, but had not taken the step to commit her life to Him to develop a personal relationship. One day I read a commitment prayer to her and asked her if she wanted to commit her life to Jesus. To my surprise she was amenable. When we finished, I sighed with relief. I could finally rest in the completeness of God's promise on her behalf. I told her, "Now Jesus has you. I'm turning you over to Him."

At a later date I asked her if she still had trouble praying. She nodded yes. This time I asked her if the difficulty was in putting her thoughts together. She confirmed. The stroke was her unrelenting battlefield. A tear collected in her eye and I responded by coaxing her to say her favorite cuss word. We laughed, hugged, and then I led her in prayer. I asked Jesus to intercede for her when she couldn't put together the words. When I finished I noticed her eyes were still tightly closed. After a minute or two she opened her eyes and indicated she wasn't finished praying. I quietly rejoiced.

Mom showed her acceptance by agreeing to go more places. She eagerly went to her weekly beauty shop appointments, accompanied her friend, Mary, and me to the movies, and she enthusiastically joined the family at local restaurants. Willingly taking advantage of out-patient rehabilitation, she gained more physical strength during transfers and worked hard to communicate during speech therapy. I never dreamed that she would progress in her recovery to this extent. She could even walk short distances under close supervision and with the aid of her walker. Her participation defied and seemed to keep at bay the depression that plagued her.

For Mom, her most apparent act of contempt for her predicament was her consistent refusal to use her call button. This hallmark of defiance emerged immediately after the stroke and continued well into a year after the stroke. When called to task, she would shake her head in disgust. However, at this juncture, she showed great strides of acceptance with her willingness to push the call button. To her credit, she now regularly used it.

Chapter 8

Endurance

As out-patient rehabilitation ended, we settled in for the long haul. Our search for a better place resolved into a comfortable apartment with kind and loving caregivers. Hopes for recovery embodied in therapy matured into the realization that what we had was all that could be. I quit struggling with expectations and enjoyed the precious time remaining. Drew and I searched to no avail for other outside activities for Mom. What she had was what we could do for her, and that would be enough. We set up a computer with solitaire and brought puzzles, our pets, and books on tape. I purchased a DVD player so that she could watch movies. On good days, we challenged Mom with a game of cards. We continued the outings to our homes and to restaurants when she agreed, and most of all, we sat with her, cried with her, laughed with her, held her hand, and apprised her of our activities.

We put a phone in Mom's living room, and if you

called she would respond with "Pretty Good." That was the only utterance she could muster on her own, so her answer to all questions was, "Pretty Good." I hooked a webcam to her computer and aimed it at her chair in the living room. After many visits from the local computer expert we managed to find free software that would monitor her. We also installed a startup procedure that would automatically start the webcam software when the computer was restarted after accidentally being unplugged, which happened regularly. That allowed me to call her on the phone when I saw that she was seated in her chair. There were good and bad points to this addition. The good was that I could see her when I was out of town and could tune in any time to see what she was doing. The bad part was that it was hard for me to watch her sit there all alone. I found myself watching her all of the time at work and had to limit my own use of the monitoring.

During this time I learned a subtle difference between endurance and perseverance. Previously for me, endurance and perseverance conjured the same picture of stoic survival: "hunkering down" to weather the storm, stamina in the face of a nightmare. My view of endurance and perseverance denoted a display of staying power, a focus on outliving the circumstances of the trial - hanging on.

After studying the biblical references to perseverance, I took note of the apparent contradiction in considering it pure joy to face trials of many kinds, because the testing of faith develops perseverance (James

1: 2-4). I guess the operative point for me was the relationship between trials of many kinds and testing of my faith. They were synonymous. During trials, my faith would be, by definition, tested. Therefore, my focus must be on my faith and in whom I believe, not the twists and turns nor the outcome of the trial. Perseverance is produced through the strength of faith. It is a noun not a verb; it is the result not the action.

The difference I uncovered was subtle but life-changing. The action I tried to perfect was to abandon my will, to humble myself with a pure heart, then to listen to the God in whom I place my faith. The trial became a forum for which I could actively develop my faith, an opportunity to trust, and a time to show the strength and truth of my beliefs. I did what I could do in the circumstances and I let the outcome go. My focus was upward not inward or outward. In the resulting mental image, I was standing on a rock instead of hanging by a thread. Controlling the result became less of an issue, and perseverance was indeed the by-product.

Calmness settled over me and we all plugged along, taking one day at a time. Mom had good days and days she seemed confused. Her eyes exposed her. Some days they were bright and alert, typical of the vibrant mother I knew, while others revealed a sad detachment common in many elderly eyes. I continued connecting, gazing deeply into her expression, stroking her face, and telling her I loved her. By staring at her mortality, I glimpsed mine as well.

Because my voice was the only audible voice between us, I took the lead in consoling both of us with the hope of my beliefs. Her way to death became my way of life. I was regularly verbalizing the fundamental tenants of my values: what I really believed about life, death, and life-after-death. I couldn't shake the eternal perspective and that wasn't a bad thing. In accompanying Mom through her decline, I saw the wisdom of the song lyrics, "I hope you get the chance to live like you are dying."

Mom's ordeal forced me to arise; to try and trust; to let go, look up, and linger; to explore, experience and evaluate; to live, love, and laugh; to face, fight, finish, and forgive. I emerged enriched, not defeated. Her dependence and inability to speak up for herself forced me to draw on my own inner strength to meet her needs. In doing so, I broke free, realized my own talents then appreciated hers. I found strength in unexpected places and discovered my own personal power.

Why had it taken me so long to find my inner capacity? I was well beyond the age of maturity, and I was equipped with plenty of family support, a doctorate degree, and accompanying accomplishments. What had kept me constrained in covert dependent thinking? I had matured in many respects while remaining inert in a very critical aspect. Although I had functioned as an adult, I was emotionally tethered with childhood thinking within the mother-daughter relationship. What should be a dynamic, evolving relationship had remained unintentionally static.

Chapter 9

Rite of Passage

Circumstances thrust Mom and me into a dramatic change of power in our mother-daughter relationship. Mom had always held the power. She stated her opinions and when she did, I took them as judgments. Her words became decrees over my reality, regardless of her intentions. I unconsciously desired her approval and was affected when she disapproved. I am not sure she realized the ripple effect of her words in my world, and I do not even think she desired that power. However, for whatever reason, I remained in the submissive role, missing the transition to equal footing. I tried not to let her opinions affect me, with very little success. In her formidable presence, I inadvertently slipped into a passive, vulnerable position.

In our family, there seemed to be a more pronounced transition for my brother into manhood than there was for me into womanhood. When Drew graduated from law school and got his first job, he occupied a position of autonomy in the mind-set of the family.

Although unspoken, it was perfectly clear to all that he became a man with all the accompanying rights and responsibilities when he embarked on his career. He had gained an independent footing in his relationship with our parents.

On the other hand, my relationship with my parents did not seem to change even through college graduation, marriage, and becoming a mother myself, at least in my perspective. My father was killed in a plane crash during the first year of my first career, so I never turned the corner to enjoy an adult relationship with him. I am not sure why I remained stuck in routine responses with Mom, and I lament the absence of clear rite of passage. Of course Mom complimented me on my accomplishments and bragged on me to friends, but I never felt on equal footing with her. I would have benefited from conversations with her recognizing changes in our relationship as I matured.

I will make it a point to bestow the blessings of an unambiguous rite of passage to my children. I hope to negotiate roles and discuss emerging relationships. Society will help with my son. Landing his first career position and taking a wife will mark his passage. There is an inherent understanding of becoming a man, and there will be opportunities to talk about it. It will be easy to recognize new boundaries established in his household. For my daughter, I hope to state the obvious and mark the changes in our relationship verbally. I hope to offer advice instead of judgments and help her realize how wonderfully capable she is in her career, encouraging the development of her inner strength, courage, and independence. I will assist her in becoming a mother and support the decisions she makes with her husband. Celebrating their growth, I will rally around both my son and my daughter. Most importantly I will talk about changes in our relationships.

Chapter 10

Suffering

Mom's decline was neither steady nor consistent, and I wrestled with my resulting feelings. By year four she had fought back from heart surgery, infection, stroke, profound anemia, kidney failure, congestive heart failure, and a broken hip. As Mom teetered with each crisis, I envisioned release from bondage. Then I would cringe in shame for thinking of liberation. I wondered whose freedom I anticipated, hers or mine. After all, I wasn't the one who was suffering - or was I? Watching her gasp for breath, writhe in pain, choke with nausea, quiver in weakness, and sigh with desperation was indeed a form of suffering, but one that seemed to pale in comparison to hers. Although I adjusted to the loss of my freedom, adopted a one-day-at-a-time attitude, released Mom to God's will and timing, I never got used to the agony of watching her suffer. Just when I thought my heart could break no more, it would break all over again.

With each release from the hospital I felt I must "gear up and cheer up" to lead the continued fight. However, with each battle Mom lost strength, and once again we had to find ways to cope with new aspects of her deteriorating condition. I strained to evaluate her care and bounced back and forth from panic to surrender to the inevitable. One day Mom felt okay, and the very next day she was grasping to survive. It got to the point that I didn't even want to share her condition with those who were kind enough to ask because I knew it would drastically change in the next moment. I was continually caught off guard with the direction Mom seemed to be going.

I greeted each day trying to determine what I could do for Mom that day and adopted the attitude that whatever I could manage, would be good enough. The good days were the days I could do something specific to help her feel better. The scary days were the helpless ones. As long as I could consult with the doctors, determine and fill her current needs, bring her a milkshake, take her for a ride, rub lotion on her legs, or whatever hit me at the time, I could manage. The hard times for me were spent in sitting next to her, unable to help as she struggled.

There is no joy in suffering for either the one in distress or the one watching. The one in misery must show courage and that was Mom's specialty. She wouldn't make eye contact during crisis. She would simply clench her fist, peer up to the sky then close her eyes, suffering in silence. Nausea or leg cramps would rob her of deep breaths, and she panted to hang on to her composure. I had the job of watching, and because she had no voice, I must watch closely for changes in her countenance in order to advocate for her. The worst was when she couldn't breathe or swallow, for neither could I.

When I thought the suffering could get no worse, it did. We finally encountered a fork in the road with two roads from which to choose, bleak and bleaker. She had a deep vein thrombosis (DVT). She bled out in her shoulder due to the blood thinning therapy for the DVT which brought us to the final stalemate. The treatment for the DVT exacerbated the bleeding. We could no longer give her blood thinners for the clot because she was bleeding out. She had very low blood counts despite many units of blood and very low blood pressure. We could stay in the hospital and continue tinkering with medicines to no avail, or we could go home with hospice. In either event, the things we were doing medically were not fixing any of her problems. She had signaled me that she wanted the IV out of her arm and when Drew asked her if she wanted anymore transfusions, she shook her head no. We left the hospital and started down the final road with hospice.

During times of suffering I wondered what I could do for her and, in turn, what anyone could do for me. Of course the same two things surfaced that I had heard from countless others. Be there and pray. The connection with another human being cannot be measured during suffering. That was the hardest thing I could give to Mom and the hardest thing to ask of another.

It meant standing shoulder-to-shoulder during the heat of anguish, watching. It helped if the person standing next to me actually understood the pain, but short of that, a mere connection with another person would do. Someone being there became the channel for bringing life and carrying agony away.

Prayer worked in tandem with presence, but was by far the more powerful of the two. Prayer meant standing in the gap, drawing God's ultimate presence to the situation. I prayed for Mom and coveted prayer for myself. Prayer bathed and abated the pain for both of us. God's presence superseded the torment, and His presence comforted. In essence during this time, my moments with Mom were centered on prayer.

It was an important epiphany for me when God spoke through a newly-acquired spiritual friend to tell me that my task during Mom's suffering was spiritual not physical. My friend told me that I was preparing Mom for the next life, mending her spirit, and weaving threads of gold for her. I was the conduit through which God was pouring His love. I was standing in the gap, bringing His presence to her along with relief. I took this cue to pray with Mom each visit. During prayer, Mom seemed to melt into a trance, and I often wondered if she nodded off to sleep. Each time she, eagerly clutched my hand while I prayed. As she relaxed, her breathing slowed, and she slipped off for a few moments. I was glad she escaped.

Often Mom would close her eyes first and begin the prayer without me. I strained to hear her words and sometimes I could perceive her spirit. We took walks in the spirit many times. We seemed to hang out in the green pastures and still waters of Psalm 23. I still felt she had difficulty getting into the spiritual without me. I asked her if she saw Holy Spirit when we prayed. She nodded her head, yes. Then I ask her if she saw Holy Spirit with others. She shook her head, no. I followed with inquiring if she saw Holy Spirit on her own. She replied with another no.

One day in the hospital when she was in a particularly critical state, I took her hand in an extended prayer. She moved into her trance-like state easily, and I settled in to declare God's word over her. She affirmed her belief in Jesus Christ and I declared the blood of Jesus covered her. We moved effortlessly together in the spirit, hand-in-hand. I paraphrased the words of Jesus, "In my father's house there are many rooms. I go to prepare a place for you. If it were not so I would have told you so." I felt like we were approaching her room in God's house. I could almost see the warm, golden light that was emanating from the room. I encouraged her to go in to look around to see if it was decorated just the way she wanted it to be.

Suddenly we were interrupted by a nurse who scurried in and out of the room. When the nurse left I looked at Mom and said, "You just barely peeked into your room in heaven, then you turned and ran out, didn't you?" She laughed aloud in agreement. "You didn't ever let go of my hand, did you?" She confirmed by laughing again.

Jesus said the Kingdom of Heaven is here, now, so I do believe there is access to the spiritual realm at any time. It was sweet to move with Mom in that dimension. At times she was reluctant, but at other times, she traveled easily. There was peace for me during those moments and her countenance indicated there was peace for her as well. Although Mom was close to her eternal home during this hospital stay, she did not make her final journey until much later.

Chapter 11

Inheritance

As I began to contemplate inheritance, it occurred to me that there were several types of inheritance. Of course there was a small material inheritance which could afford opportunities, but I do not consider it to be the sum total of my inheritance. For me, a greater bequest was being forced to break away from the shadow of my parents and realize my own power. My spiritual legacy developed as well, and I stepped into the middle of my beliefs and began to live them. Mom's struggle became the context in which I realized my personal and spiritual heritage.

Personally, I noticed unmistakable traces of Mom emerge in my own behaviors. I felt her unsinkable spirit embrace me each time we faced another challenge, and I reached down within myself to find the positive spin on the situation. I connected my reliance on established routines to her belief that routines promoted healthy living. Before Mom's illness, I couldn't remember a morning when my Mom was not dressed and ready to greet the day with her "best foot forward" and her bed "made." Now I was exhibiting those same behaviors. Mom hated to get into an unmade bed and sincerely believed that "how you looked affected how you felt." Other things could be out of order in her house, but her bed was made and she was meticulously groomed. I remember when I was sick she would allow me enough time in bed to recuperate, but when she sensed a hint of recovery she would encourage me to overcome with, "Get dressed and it will make you feel better!" Those memories replayed in my mind as I dressed and made up my bed.

Routines seeped into the texture of my family as I watched my daughter incorporate predictable eating and sleeping routines for her children. According to Mom, babies needed routines to be healthy and adults needed routines to be productive. As a part of Mom's morning routine, she cheerfully greeted us each morning with, "Rise and shine! Daylight is burning!" Although she tolerated the times when we ignored schedules and slept late, it was not in her nature to waste time or anything else. After a time she would invariably wake us with, "Are you going to sleep your life away?" I was surprised at the number of times I heard Mom's voice in the course of my day now and noted the unmistakable impact of her attitudes on my personal heritage.

Of course there is a family inheritance as well which is molded from group experiences and defines who we are as a group. Our family had an all-for-one, one-for-all mentality that was developed around the dinner table when I was little and which was led by my father. For example, I can remember family discussions in which my daddy emphasized the need to conserve our family finances. One way we could all contribute was by turning off the lights when we left a room. If everyone participated we would be able to provide for each other's needs. Braces for my teeth were considered by the family council and we agreed as a group to each make adjustments to fill that need. Mom maintained this spirit by buying for the grandkids based on needs even if it meant unequal disbursement.

Loyalty was also a part of our family DNA. In diffusing disputes, Mom would declare, "You don't treat your brother (sister) that way." Her voice carried a tone that demanded a level of respect and unconditional love based on being related. Likewise she modeled honor for siblings by tenderly taking care of her brother and sister despite their differences until they died. She consistently sacrificed her time and personal amenities for the benefit of family members. "Family" was a term that embodied her highest regard.

Esteem was fashioned in the kitchen. Family gatherings were characterized by home-cooked meals, especially the desserts. Mom excelled in making us feel special by preparing our favorite foods with tender loving care. She spent countless hours in the kitchen throughout her life to provide exceptional and memorable family gatherings, after which she would wipe the sweat from her face and joyously remark, "It doesn't get any better than this."

Our family also played games together. Our favorite games were a variety of card games with healthy competition. Little ones were encouraged to participate but were afforded little slack. You had to learn quickly to survive. Our most memorable times were when we drew numbers for teams to play *Catch Phrase*. We did this because no one wanted Mom on their team. This game required one person on a team to come up with clues to prompt the team to say the *Catch Phrase*. I don't think I have ever laughed as hard as we did when Mom would sit silently as the timer ticked down, unable to say a word. She would stare at the phrase, incapable of mustering a clue as her team hurled wild guesses. The other team would roll in the floor with laughter. Although she was a consistent winner at cards she was dead weight for her team on "catch phrase."

Mom was always there in my times of need. Throughout my life, she dropped what she was doing when I needed her. The most memorable example was when she appeared at my door in record time when I was unexpectedly brought home from the hospital a day early with my first child. I called her in tears not knowing what to do with this new baby and before I knew it, she was there to hold my hand and my baby. Later she arrived to pack me up and move me home after my divorce. Countless times, she dropped what she was doing and came to my rescue when, as a single mom, I had to work and I had no day care.

Our family heritage is one of loyalty and unconditional acceptance mixed with fun, competition, and fabulous food. We played together and we showed up for one another in times of need.

I'm not sure I could recognize my full inheritance until I discharged emotional interference. I had to break free to gain my personal inheritance to recognize my spiritual and family inheritance. Fortunately I was able to recognize and confirm Mom as a fellow sojourner. Inherently, parents have a vested interest in their children and are the approximation of unconditional love we experience here on earth. Most are flawed. I had the opportunity to treasure the time with Mom despite all of our imperfections. I was able to explore the territory and realize my own strength and identity in the exploration. I found power to withstand and overcome perceived injustices.

I have and will make mistakes in my children's eyes. I hope they view my mistakes as mistakes and not personal wounds. I hope they find their Mom and in doing so find their own heritage.

Epilogue

It has been over three years since Mom passed and since I have approached this journal. It has taken some time to recover from Mom's final years. The suffering I reported previously did not prove to be her last. She was released from the hospital on hospice and eventually set a record as being one of their longest living patients. Mom lived another two plus years. Only now can I return here to put the finishing touches on the story.

When we brought Mom home from the hospital that last time, I bought her many new housecoats and pajamas, equipping her for her last days in bed, never dreaming she would gain the strength to get out of bed. She was so weak from bleeding out in her shoulder that I never expected her to improve. We hired extra help for her and "hunkered down" yet again. Mom did rally, gaining the strength to somewhat resume the routine we had established.

At the news of my first grandson's arrival in another city, I installed Skype and taught the staff in the facility how to conduct online video phone calls. I was so comforted to be able to show Mom her new great grandson and my face as well during the long stay with my daughter at the birth of her son. Mom lived long enough to see his brother, Charles, being born twenty short months later as well.

Once again, there were key people who entered our lives to make a difference. Elizabeth was Mom's treasured companion during the last years. Carol, an elementary school friend of mine, also graced this time period. As hospice volunteer, Carol ran across Mom's name in the list of hospice clients, so she gladly took Mom under her wing. Carol lost her dad early in life as well, and I can still remember the day she showed up when my dad was killed to comfort me. Nothing defines effective comfort like common experiences. She knew what I was going through, so when she hugged me, I was able to transfer some of the burden. Interestingly enough, Carol lost her Mom to a debilitating stroke as well, and her mom was a good friend of my mother. Once again, Carol was on the spot to share my load with Mom. There is no better friend than that.

Carol had many talks with Mom concerning death that I just could not have. Mom and I talked a lot about heaven, God, Jesus, eternity, and her salvation, but Mom just couldn't entertain a conversation about death with me. Carol reported Mom's fears to me, and we talked about how to address them. We had various chaplains and prayer warriors pray with Mom. She seemed to be comforted each time.

One Sunday afternoon shortly before she died, I arrived ready to spend some time with Mom. We worked puzzles most Sunday afternoons but this time I found Mom sitting in her chair with tears in her eyes. I got down on my knees in front of her, gazed deeply into her eyes, and asked her the usual questions about pain and discomfort. I discerned that she was not in pain, did not need anything, but was just sad. Most of the time, I could put a cheerful spin on the situation, but the look in her eyes drew me into her plight. I burst into tears myself and sat in her lap with my head on her shoulder, wrapped in her one-armed embrace. She held me for a while and then I moved her onto the couch where I could hold her. I held her all afternoon and we let it all out. Both of us sobbed uncontrollably. I tried to compose myself, but I was no match for the tidal waves of emotion flooding through the gates that had opened.

In retrospect, Mom knew what was coming. She knew her time was short, and in my heart of hearts, I did too. About a week later Mom started declining rapidly. Carol and I had talked about how Carol's mom would not die in Carol's presence. Although Carol kept a vigil over her mom, her mom waited until Carol was out of the room to pass. Carol suspected the same was true for Mom. She said Mom would not leave me. Drew and I had taken round the clock shifts in her last days and I was going to stay the night on the day Mom died. Carol showed up to relieve me and told me to go home to get some rest. She assured me that she would call me the moment things changed. Sure enough about 3 in the morning Carol called me to come. By the time Drew and I got there, Mom was gone. I guess Mom's passing when I was gone was her final gift because she knew neither of us could say goodbye. Somehow I knew that our time cradling each other on the couch was our goodbye.

I found Mom in the midst of losing her, gained strength in my most helpless moments, and discovered hope in discouraging circumstances. As I reflect on the irony, I see the wisdom of paradox, the logic of contradiction, and the balance in opposing forces. I grew up in the shadow of Mom's strong personality, struggling for her illusive approval, bound in my submissive role. As I matured, I exerted myself but never broke free. It took the agonizing stages of losing her to finally discover her inner being and in turn my own identity. Without tragic events we would have never breached the chasm created by routine responses. I would have never known her or discovered myself. In her final days, I sought connection to her, not liberation from her; extension of our time together, not completion of it. I wanted to linger in the uncertainty to discover fully the depths our mother-daughter bond. It was a gut-wrenching process I learned to embrace.

It's ironic that the time in life when I communicated the most with my Mom was when she was she was unable to speak. I wouldn't trade that for an equivalent amount of time locked in the communication patterns we maintained while she was able to speak. My rite of passage, which would typically be characterized by conversations, was accomplished with non-verbal exchanges. It is my hope that sharing my reflections will

Epilogue

encourage those experiencing similar situations to dig deep into the faces of their loved ones, linger in the intimate moments, break out of routine responses, and seize the moment to communicate.

Works Cited

Dawson, Joy. *Forever ruined for the ordinary: The adventure of hearing and obeying God's voice.* Nashville: Thomas Nelson Publishers, 2001. Print.

www.ingramcontent.com/pod-product-compliance
Lightning Source LLC
Chambersburg PA
CBHW052028290426
44112CB00014B/2432